What's in this book

This book belongs to

_____

美食节 Food festival

学习内容 Contents

沟通 Communication

说说食物和饮料

Talk about food and drinks

背景介绍：

学校举行美食节，同学们都兴高采烈地参与活动。

生词 New words

★ 面条	noodle
★ 面包	bread
★ 汽水	soft drink
★ 杯子	cup, glass
★ 渴	thirsty
★ 汤	soup
★ 冰箱	refrigerator
★ 都	all
筷子	chopsticks
炒饭	fried rice
饺子	dumpling
准备	to prepare
餐馆	restaurant
欢迎	to welcome
碗	bowl

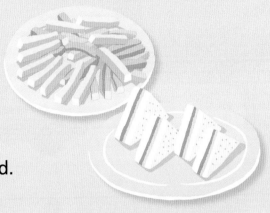

句式 Sentence patterns

同学们都准备了不同的美食。
Schoolmates all prepared different kinds of food.

这些都是我爸爸做的。
These all were made by my father.

跨学科学习 Project

认识五种基本味道，并尝味道，猜食物
Learn the five basic tastes and try the blindfolded taste test

文化 Cultures

中式就餐礼仪
Chinese dining etiquette

参考答案：
1 Yes, we hold a food festival every year./No, but we have tea parties.
2 My favourite food is pizza/spaghetti/fried rice.
3 I can see sandwiches, fries, buns, hamburgers, pizza, fried rice, soup, fish and chocolates.

Get ready

1 Has your school ever held a food festival?

2 What is your favourite food?

3 What food can you see here?

zhǔn bèi
准备

dōu
都

"都"用于动
或形容词前。

故事大意：
学校举行美食节，大家都从家里准备了食物
带到学校一起分享。

今天，学校举行美食节，同学们都准备了不同的美食。

参考问题和答案：

1　What event is the school having? (The school is having a food festival.)

2　Who do you think prepared all the food? (The students prepared the food.)

参考问题和答案：

1 What have Ethan and Ivan prepared?
  (They have prepared some bread and soda.)
2 Why do they have a banner of a restaurant? (They want to show
  that their booth is just like a restaurant.)
3 What are Ethan and Ivan saying? ('Welcome to our restaurant!')

伊森和艾文拿着面包和汽水，说：
"欢迎大家来我们的餐馆！"

高兴地迎接他人时，我们说"欢迎！"或者"欢迎……！"

jiǎo zi
饺子

miàn tiáo
面条

参考问题和答案：

1 What have Ling Ling and Hao Hao prepared? (They have prepared some noodles and dumplings.)

2 Why does Elsa look excited? (She is excited about the dumplings. She likes them.)

3 Do you like noodles or dumplings? (Yes, they taste good./I don't know. I have not tried them before.)

玲玲准备了面条和饺子，爱莎看见了，说："你的食物应该很好吃！"

参考问题和答案：

1 What has Elsa prepared? (She has prepared some fried rice and a pot of soup.)
2 What is Elsa doing? (She is asking Ling Ling to try the fried rice and the soup.)
3 Do you like fried rice and soup? (Yes, I like them both./I like fried rice but not hot soup.)

tāng
汤

chǎo fàn
炒饭

"你们试试炒饭和蔬菜汤，这些都是我爸爸做的。"爱莎又说。

kě
渴

bīng xiāng
冰箱

参考问题和答案：

1 How does Hao Hao look? Is he thirsty? (He is sweating and h
looks thirsty.

2 What do you think Hao Hao is asking the others? (He is aski
if they are thirsty as well.)

3 Where is Hao Hao storing his drinks? (In a small refrigerator

浩浩说："你们渴吗？喝我做的果汁
吧！果汁在冰箱里面，很新鲜。"

参考问题和答案：

1 What utensils are next to Elsa's fried rice? (Some bowls, some chopsticks and a big spoon.)

2 What is Ethan asking? (He is asking if anyone has a glass.)

3 How do the children look? Why? (They look surprised because they forget to bring glasses.)

bēi zi
杯子

wǎn
碗

kuài zi
筷子

"这里只有碗、刀、叉、筷子和盘子，谁带了杯子？"伊森问。哎呀，大家都忘了！

Let's think 提醒学生回忆故事，观察第 5 至 8 页。

1 Recall the story. Match the food prepared by the children.

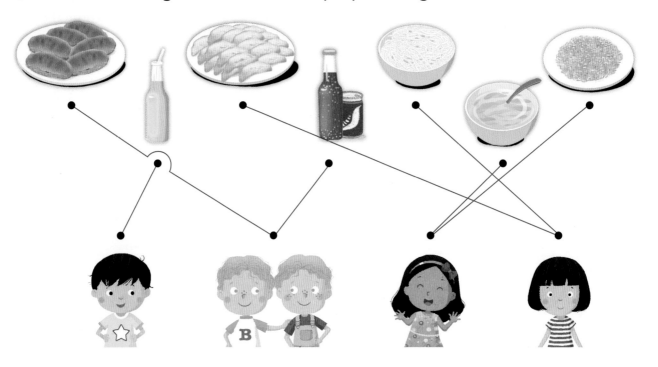

2 What will you prepare if your school holds a food festival? Draw your ideas below and tell your friend.

我要做……

我和妈妈一起准备蔬菜水果汁。

我和妈妈做蛋糕。

New words

延伸活动：
让学生尽量用生词看图说话。参考表述：他们在餐馆工作，服务员说："欢迎！"/
这家餐馆有很多不同的食物，你喜欢面条还是炒饭？/浩浩和玲玲都渴了，他们要
喝冰箱里的果汁。/浩浩和玲玲用筷子吃面条和饺子。玲玲的杯子里还有果汁。

1 Learn the new words.

2 Point to the above words randomly and ask your friend to say them.

听听说说 Listen and say

1 Listen and circle the correct letters.

1 男孩要了什么果汁？

   a 葡萄汁

   (b) 苹果汁

   c 香蕉汁

2 男孩还要了什么？

   a 炒饭

   b 饺子

   (c) 蔬菜汤

3 男孩没有要什么？

   a 面条

   b 面包

   (c) 汉堡包

这个音频较长，信息比较多，在做题前，提醒学生边听音频边做一些笔记。

2 Look at the pictures. Listen to the story

跑步真累！我饿了，我们一起去吃午饭吧。

太好了！因为我也饿了。

这些食物都不健康。你别天天吃。

那我们吃什么？

第二题参考问题和答案：
Why do Elsa and Hao Hao decide to go to the Chinese restaurant? (Because the dumplings and the noodles there taste good.)

第一题录音稿：

服务员：您好，请问几位？
男孩：　两位。
服务员：请坐。请问你们想要些什么？
男孩：　我们要一杯汽水、一杯果汁、一碗面条和一个面包。
服务员：请问要苹果汁还是葡萄汁？

男孩：　苹果汁。
服务员：好的，还有什么吗？
男孩：　再来一碗蔬菜汤吧。
服务员：好的，请等等，这些已经在准备中了。
男孩：　谢谢。
服务员：不客气！

你想吃什么？

我想吃汉堡包和薯条，喝汽水。

我们去公园北边的中国餐馆吧，那里的饺子和面条都很好吃。

好啊，我们快走吧！

3 Complete the sentences and role-play with your friend.

a 筷子　b 面包　c 都
d 碗　　e 冰箱　f 渴

你_f_吗？家里没有汽水，
只有果汁，在_e_里。

_b_和蔬菜汤，我_c_很喜欢。

快来吃晚饭吧，面条在
_d_里，_a_也准备好了。

Task

提醒学生用本课生词及已有中文食物名称如三明治、鸡蛋、汉堡包、薯条、蔬菜、米饭等来完成此题。

Draw and tell your friend what you ate yesterday.

Game

玩游戏前，可先与学生复习一些食物名称，然后让学生从下图圈出食物生词，看谁圈得又多又快。

Find and circle food words. Play with your friend to see who can circle the most food words.

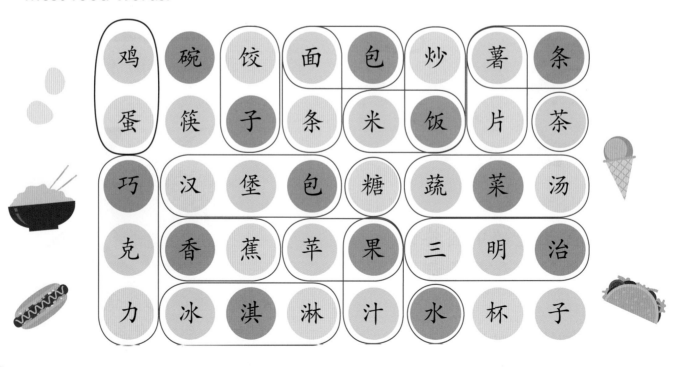

Chant

说唱第一段第 1 至 4 句时，学生可配合歌词做相应的烹饪动作；
说唱第二段第 1 至 5 句时，学会做相应的进食动作。

05 Listen and say.

我准备炒饭，
你准备饺子，
他准备面条，
她准备面包。
今天学校美食节，
大家都带来美食。

我爱吃炒饭，
你爱吃饺子，
他爱吃面条，
她爱吃面包。
大家都爱喝果汁，
大家都爱蔬菜汤。

生活用语 Daily expressions

欢迎你来学校！
Welcome to our school!

准备一下。
Getting ready.

15

写一写 Write

1 Trace and write the characters.

单一结构

面 一 厂 厂 币 而 而 面 面

包 一 勹 勹 包

面	包	面	包
面	包		

半包围结构

杯 一 十 十 才 木 杙 杯

子 フ 了 子

左右结构

杯	子	杯	子
杯	子		

单一结构

2 Write and say.

这是我们做的面包，很好吃！

在我的生日会，我准备了纸杯子，大家一起喝果汁。

3 Fill in the blanks with the correct words. Colour the hats using the same colours.

他们
粉色

好吃
蓝色

面包
黄色

工作
绿色

我的爸爸在 面包 店 工作 ，
从星期一到星期六，他天天都
很早起床去上班。

一天，爸爸带我去看他
上班的地方。那里还有很多
叔叔、阿姨， 他们 都会做
面包 ，那些 面包 都很 好吃 。

拼音输入法 Pinyin input

Number the sentences to make a meaningful paragraph. Then type the correct paragraph.

2 我们吃了炒饭、面条和饺子。

4 我觉得这家餐馆的饭菜很好
吃，我还想去。

1 星期天，我们一家人去北京餐
馆吃饭了。

3 我们还喝了果汁和蔬菜汤。

告诉学生应先找段落中心句（"星期天，我们……"）；然后找具体描述中心句的内容（"我们吃了……"和"我们还……"），并从关键词"还"得出该句应放在后面；最后找段落总结句（"我觉得这家餐馆……"）。

 Connections

Cultures

延伸活动：
老师介绍完中国进餐礼仪需注意的事项后，可问问学生在本国的进餐礼仪中有哪些需要注意的地方。告诉学生培养良好的进餐礼仪的重要性，因为它能反映出个人的素养。

1 Different cultures have different dining etiquettes. Learn some of the do's and don'ts in Chinese dining.

Let the elders sit first before taking a seat yourself. This is a gesture of politeness.

Let the elders eat first, or wait for them to say 'Let's eat.' before you start to eat. This is showing your respect for the elders.

Do not lick the tips of the chopsticks. It is impolite.

Do not stick the chopsticks straight up in rice. It is not lucky.

Do not tap your rice bowl with chopsticks. It is a sign of begging for food.

2 Learn and practise how to use chopsticks. It is easy!

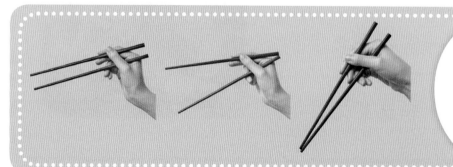

Hold the chopsticks in one hand. Use your index and middle fingers to move the upper stick up and down.

提醒学生握筷子时，两支筷子的头要对齐，夹食物的效果才会更好。

18

让学生说说自己喜欢的食物的味道，然后问问他们是否知道我们是怎样尝出不同的味道的，进而介绍下面的内容。

1 Do you know how many tastes humans can sense? Learn about them.

Taste buds on our tongues are able to differentiate different tastes.

舌头
tongue

味蕾
taste buds

味蕾是味觉的感受器，可以品尝出不同味道。人的舌头上约有一万多个味蕾。每一个味蕾都能够感受到所有的基本味觉。所以，舌头各个区域对于不同味觉的感受都是相差无几的。

The sensation of taste includes five basic tastes:

吃薯条

咸 salty

甜 sweet
吃糖

苦 bitter
喝药水

鲜 umami
喝汤

酸 sour

吃柠檬

2 Try the blindfolded taste test with your friends and see whose tongue is more sensitive.

这是什么？

这应该是巧克力，它有一点儿苦，又有一点儿甜。

除以上食物外，学生可多试一些别的食物或饮料。

游戏方法：
学生先独立默读整个对话并完成填空。然后七人一组练习对话，模仿真实的晚餐情景。最后各小组轮流在全班面前表演，看哪组的说话最流利最有感情。

1 Look at the picture and draw your face in the blank circles. Write the characters. Role-play with your friends.

欢迎你来……

谢谢大家，我今天很高兴！

大家都有杯子、碗和筷子了吗？

你们渴吗？汽水从冰箱里拿来了。

今天的面条、炒饭和蔬菜汤看起来都很好吃。

你会不会写 bread 的中文字？ 面 包

我最喜欢吃饺子了。

评核方法：
学生两人一组，互相考察评价表内单词和句子的听说读写。交际沟通部分由老师朗读要求，学生再互相对话。
如果达到了某项技能要求，则用色笔将星星或小辣椒涂色。

2 Work with your friend. Colour the stars and the chillies.

Words	说	读	写
面包	☆	☆	☆
面条	☆	☆	🌶
汽水	☆	☆	🌶
杯子	☆	☆	☆
渴	☆	☆	🌶
汤	☆	☆	🌶
冰箱	☆	☆	🌶
都	☆	☆	🌶
筷子	☆	🌶	🌶
炒饭	☆	🌶	🌶
饺子	☆	🌶	🌶

Words and sentences	说	读	写
准备	☆	🌶	🌶
餐馆	☆	🌶	🌶
欢迎	☆	🌶	🌶
碗	☆	🌶	🌶
同学们都准备了不同的美食。	☆	☆	🌶
这些都是我爸爸做的。	☆	☆	🌶

Talk about food and drinks	☆

3 What does your teacher say?

My teacher says ...

评核建议：
根据学生课堂表现，分别给予"太棒了！(Excellent!)"、
"不错！(Good!)"或"继续努力！(Work harder!)"的
评价，再让学生圈出上方对应的表情，以记录自己的学
习情况。

分享 Sharing

延伸活动：
1 学生用手遮盖英文，读中文单词，并思考单词意思；
2 学生用手遮盖中文单词，看着英文说出对应的中文单□
3 学生两人一组，尽量运用中文单词分角色复述故事。

Words I remember

面条	miàn tiáo	noodle
面包	miàn bāo	bread
汽水	qì shuǐ	soft drink
杯子	bēi zi	cup, glass
渴	kě	thirsty
汤	tāng	soup
冰箱	bīng xiāng	refrigerator
都	dōu	all
筷子	kuài zi	chopsticks
炒饭	chǎo fàn	fired rice
饺子	jiǎo zi	dumpling
准备	zhǔn bèi	to prepare
餐馆	cān guǎn	restaurant
欢迎	huān yíng	to welcome
碗	wǎn	bowl

Other words

举行	jǔ xíng	to hold
美食节	měi shí jié	food festival
美食	měi shí	gourmet food
食物	shí wù	food
试	shì	to try
新鲜	xīn xiān	fresh
刀	dāo	knife
叉	chā	fork
盘子	pán zi	dish
哎呀	āi ya	oh (a kind of modal particle)
要	yào	to need, to want
舌头	shé tou	tongue
味蕾	wèi lěi	taste buds
甜	tián	sweet
咸	xián	salty
酸	suān	sour
苦	kǔ	bitter
鲜	xiān	umami

OXFORD
UNIVERSITY PRESS

Oxford University Press is a department of the University of Oxford.
It furthers the University's objective of excellence in research, scholarship,
and education by publishing worldwide. Oxford is a registered trade mark of
Oxford University Press in the UK and in certain other countries

Published in Hong Kong by
Oxford University Press (China) Limited
39th Floor, One Kowloon, 1 Wang Yuen Street, Kowloon Bay,
Hong Kong

Illustrated by Ah Lun, Anne Lee, Emily Chan, KY Chan and Wildman

Photographs for reproduction permitted by Dreamstime.com

China National Publications Import & Export (Group) Corporation is an authorized distributor of
Oxford Elementary Chinese.

Please contact content@cnpiec.com.cn or 86-10-65856782

ISBN: 978-0-19-082312-2

10 9 8 7 6 5 4 3 2

Teacher's Edition
ISBN: 978-0-19-082324-5

10 9 8 7 6 5 4 3 2